"The spirit of

Some recollections of the artist and the painting

Henry Kelsey Devereux

Alpha Editions

This edition published in 2024

ISBN : 9789361473739

Design and Setting By
Alpha Editions
www.alphaedis.com
Email - info@alphaedis.com

As per information held with us this book is in Public Domain.
This book is a reproduction of an important historical work. Alpha Editions uses the best technology to reproduce historical work in the same manner it was first published to preserve its original nature. Any marks or number seen are left intentionally to preserve its true form.

Contents

Preface .... - 1 -

Archibald M. Willard a brief sketch .... - 2 -

The Fifer .... - 8 -

The Drummer Boy .... - 10 -

An Early Account .... - 14 -

Preliminary Sketches and Replicas .... - 17 -

Preface

Nearly fifty years have passed since Archibald M. Willard painted "The Spirit of '76." Mr. Willard has passed, and so have all who were intimately connected with its creation, except myself. Probably no painting, the creation of an American artist, has received such wide and continuous interest and attention as this patriotic painting. Many times during the last quarter of a century, I have been urged to record my recollections of Willard and my association with this historical painting. Many times I have been asked for information which did not come under my personal observation. As the years pass, this demand for information has become more insistent and more urgent. This little volume has been prepared partly to meet this demand, but more especially to accede to the oft-repeated requests of my family and friends.

These requests for information have not always been confined to my own experiences. Therefore, the more fully to meet the wishes of my family and friends, to my own personal recollections I have added a brief sketch of the artist, of Hugh Mosher the fifer, and Mr. Ryder's own account of the conception and purpose of the artist, written many years ago and now difficult to find. I have also added a few words regarding the extant original sketches and the Replica of 1912.

H. K. D.

January 1926

Archibald M. Willard
a brief sketch

ARCHIBALD M. WILLARD

at the age of forty, when he painted the "Spirit of '76"

A brief sketch of Archibald M. Willard and the Spirit of '76

"The Spirit of '76" is the best known painting produced by an American, and at the same time one of the most inspiring works of art ever issued in America. It may not conform to any orthodox school of painting or possess the fine points of technique that some critics demand, but as an inspiration of patriotism, I doubt if any painting has had as wide and continuous influence as "The Spirit of '76." It has been reproduced in one form and another millions of times, by almost every available process—chromo-lithography, steel-engraving, half-tone, and the various color processes. It is perhaps available in more homes than any other American painting, either framed or in magazines, printed books, school histories, calendars, posters, etc. Many a patriotic parade has included the famous trio of this painting.

Although the painting is so universally known, it is surprising that so little authentic printed material is available either on the artist himself or the story of the creation of this, his most celebrated work.

Archibald M. Willard, the painter of "The Spirit of '76" was born in Bedford, Ohio, August 22, 1836. His father, the Reverend Samuel Willard, was a Baptist minister and a Vermonter. In the home was grandfather Willard, between whom and the young artist there grew to be a strong bond of understanding and sympathy. The grandfather, a relative of General Stark and a soldier of the Revolutionary War, was one of the Green Mountain boys who was at the surrender of General Burgoyne. Grandfather and grandson spent much time together in rambles through the then picturesque Bedford glens. The rugged surroundings appealed to young Willard's artistic sense. The old man figured often in the boy's cartoons. Many a tree was stripped of its outer bark to produce a smooth surface upon which with red chalk and charred embers the young artist produced savages of hideous mien. As frequently happens with young artists, young Willard, did not receive much encouragement from the Willard family, perhaps because every smooth surface of wall, barn-door, board fence, etc., bore evidence to the budding genius.

For varying periods, the family were located at Kent, Salem, Aurora, Mantua, and La Grange. When Willard was a lad of seventeen, the family moved to Wellington, Lorain county, Ohio. At the outbreak of the Civil War, Willard enlisted in the Eighty-sixth Ohio Regiment. While with his regiment at Cumberland Gap, he painted several pictures of the surrounding country. These were photographed and many of the photographs were sold to his comrades.

With the close of the Civil War, Archibald M. Willard, then a sturdy young man, returned to Wellington, together with his close companion, Hugh Mosher. Both had served faithfully and well. Willard had become a non-commissioned officer. He secured employment in the shop of E. S. Tripp, a wheelwright and wagon-maker. The old shop still stands at Wellington. Willard's original job was to paint the wagons. From the mere painting of the wagons he gradually passed to decorating the wagons artistically, and finally to decorating, with woodland and animal scenes, a number of gaudy circus chariots. He did this work so artistically that "Tripp's wagons" became known all over that part of the country. There was coöperation between the two men, for apart from the artistic painting, the wagons themselves were sturdily and well-built. Willard's artistic temperament carried him beyond mere commercial painting. He began painting pictures on the wagon boxes. These were so well executed that they created much comment. He gradually became so elaborate in these, that his employer, Mr. Tripp, had to restrain him. Undoubtedly the interest created by these paintings sold many a wagon for their builder and advertised him in a most unusual way. If any of these Willard-decorated-Tripp-wagons were now available, they would bring a price far in excess of the cost of the wagons themselves.

While working at his trade as wagon painter, Willard devoted all his spare time, energy, and what little money he could save to the study of painting on canvas. He had a very decided sense of humor and nearly all of his earlier subjects are of a humorous character. It was early in the seventies that he painted the first two pictures from which he received compensation. These were the outcome of a request by his employer's daughter asking him to paint a picture for her. "Pluck number One" was the result. It depicts a dog hitched to a little wagon, a boy driving, and his baby sister in the wagon with him. The dog takes off the road in chase of a rabbit, and the little boy desperately trying to stop him. A wreck follows where the rabbit jumps a log, but the youthful occupant clinging to the lines, and the little sister, escapes unhurt.

In Cleveland at this time was a photographer and art dealer named J. F. Ryder. This painting came to his attention with other early productions by Willard. The astute Ryder quickly recognized the quaint humor and natural ability displayed in these early pictures. Willard thereupon painted a sequel to "Pluck" which he entitled "Pluck number Two." Mr. Ryder had these two paintings reproduced in color by chromo-lithography. They became two of the most popular pictures of their day. They sold at ten dollars the pair. Many thousands were sold. This proved to be the beginning of a long and profitable business acquaintance and lasting friendship between Willard and Ryder. The proceeds from the sale of these pictures permitted Willard to take an art course in the studio of J. D. Eaton, of New York. This was in 1873.

"YANKEE DOODLE"

Willard's original conception for the humorous painting submitted to J. F. Ryder. From this, the "Spirit of '76," with its far-reaching inspiration, was finally evolved

Following this, Willard painted among other things a picture which he called "Yankee Doodle." It was an ordinary sized canvas and delineated a Fourth of July celebration in a country village. An old man in the center beating a drum, with a younger man on each side, the one with a drum, the other with a fife. The surroundings and background were rural. This painting was finished a few months prior to the opening of the Centennial Exposition of 1876 at Philadelphia. When Mr. Ryder saw the picture, he immediately conceived the idea of changing the subject from humorous to patriotic, and Willard concurred in the idea.

Contrary to a rather general belief, "The Spirit of '76" was not painted for exhibition at the Centennial. At that period there was a general and widespread spirit of patriotism and the days of the Revolutionary War were especially before the people of this country. Mr. Ryder had this prominently in mind and for this reason he suggested to Willard the painting of this picture that reproductions therefrom might be made and a large number of these reproductions sold generally throughout the country and particularly at the Centennial. It was not sent to the Centennial until many of these colored reproductions had been distributed, and a large popular interest in the painting had arisen. It was then, on special request made by those in charge of the Centennial that the original painting itself was sent to the Exposition.

Mr. Ryder suggested that the title be "Yankee Doodle" and under this title "The Spirit of '76" was at first known. He left the conception and development of the painting to Willard's imagination.

At that early period after the Civil War, when the training days of the militia system had practically gone to pieces, the various companies were expected to go into camp for three days each year. These days had become a neighborhood picnic. Uniforms were seldom in evidence. There were few guns or swords. There were, however, always the flag, the fife, and the drum. Willard had this idea prominently before him. He slashed into outline various charcoal attempts, but the lines would not fall or respond as he wanted them to. The real idea as to what Yankee Doodle and the men who fifed it and drummed it, stood for, eventually began to thrust itself persistently into the pencil points. Willard daily became more enthused over the patriotic features to be delineated. His early days of marching and fighting under the stars and stripes helped greatly in stirring his patriotic enthusiasm, which later was put upon and filled the completed canvas.

While Willard was engaged in painting this picture, his father, who was posing as his central figure, became critically ill. He did not live to see the finished painting. When Willard was told that his father was soon to pass away, all thoughts of a humorous picture faded from his mind. He decided to paint his father as he really was.

After Willard became acquainted with Mr. Ryder, at Ryder's suggestion, Willard moved to Cleveland. He used as a studio, a small room on the fourth floor of what used to be the Union National Bank Building located at Euclid Avenue and what was then Hickox Alley, Cleveland, Ohio. From this time on Willard spent almost his entire life in Cleveland.

This little studio had a northern exposure, and he was artist enough, even then, to realize the value of the northern light. His canvas when stretched was taller than himself. His idea had become a big one and nothing but life-size would do for the figures to be used. He followed the general idea of his first picture, "Yankee Doodle or a Fourth of July Celebration" but the spirit of the whole was changed. The old man in the center was Willard's own father, a tall, straight, powerful man, with flowing white locks yet the figure of a man of thirty, without coat, bare-headed, his white hair blowing in the breeze, his shirt sleeves loose, marching forward with a step as firm and unhesitating as the grim and determined look on his face. The face of the old man shows features which could be kind, but now set like flint in the face of the enemy—filled with the courage of a man who has put character, and thought, and prayer into the music through which he utters his patriotic purpose. Perhaps there is a bit of humor in the figure of the fifer—it could not be otherwise—for it is a portrait of the fifer of

Wellington, Hugh Mosher. While depicting his humorous face with its puckered mouth, there is the same air of determination in the figure, the eyes, and the forward step, that so mark the picture of the old man. In these characters one sees the spirit of men who will stand and play until they die, or by their contagious heroism will turn the tide of battle.

As already stated, for the first few years the painting was known under the title of "Yankee Doodle." While the picture was on exhibition in Boston, Mr. Brainerd, who had charge of the exhibition, suggested changing the title to "Yankee Doodle, or the Spirit of '76." This suggestion was made because at that time in Boston there was a public character, a half-wit, who was commonly known about the city as "Yankee Doodle." In some curious way, the painting and this half-wit were being confused in the public mind. This change of title was adopted. Finally "Yankee Doodle" was dropped entirely and the painting has since been known under the title of "The Spirit of '76."

The Fifer

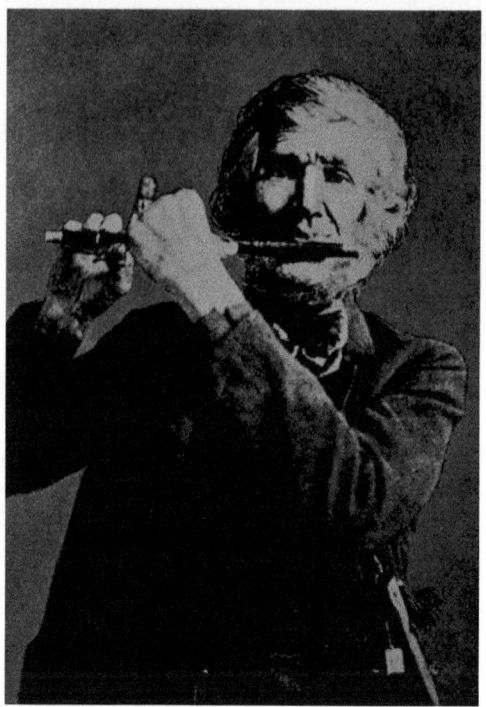

HUGH MOSHER

who posed as the fifer. From an original photograph made by William F. Sawtelle of Wellington, Ohio

The Fifer—Hugh Mosher

When Archibald M. Willard returned home from service in the Civil War, there came back with him to Wellington his comrade, Hugh Mosher. Mr. Willard first became acquainted with Mosher after the family moved to Wellington. They soon became close and lifelong friends. Their service in the Civil War, in which they were comrades, more closely cemented this friendship.

Hugh Mosher was born at Perry, Lake county, Ohio, January twenty-ninth, 1819, and died at Brighton, Ohio, August fifteenth, 1892. His father served in the War of 1812, and his grandfather had served in the Revolutionary War. He himself enlisted for the Civil War, and became a fifer in Company H, Forty-third Infantry Regiment, Ohio Volunteers. He never fully recovered from the effects of his army hardships.

He was a tall and well built man, over six feet in height. In appearance he suggested a typical frontiersman of the Daniel Boone or Simon Girty type.

Hugh Mosher (or Mosier as it is sometimes wrongly spelled) who posed as the fifer, spent most of his life in Wellington, Ohio. Returning from the Civil War, he again took up his farmwork. He was a celebrated performer on the fife, and his fame had spread throughout the surrounding country. He was probably the best fifer in northern Ohio. It is said of him that he would rather fife than eat. He carried this little instrument with him wherever he went and delighted to play whenever chance offered. No patriotic gathering in or near Wellington was considered complete without Mosher and his fife. He was intensely patriotic, and even in his last illness deeply regretted being unable to attend the celebration of the Fourth of July in his home town of Wellington.

He spent considerable time posing for Mr. Willard, and many photographs of him were taken by Mr. William F. Sawtelle, a photographer of Wellington, for use in Willard's painting. Willard, however, could not get satisfactory photographs of Hugh Mosher. This was before the day of the quick-acting shutter. The cap of the camera could not be operated quickly enough to get satisfactory expression. For this reason, poor Hugh Mosher had to go to Willard's studio and pose. In order to get the proper expression, Mosher not only had to pose, but had to continue fifing all the time he was posing. Willard had a habit of calling attention to the peculiar way in which Mosher held his fife—with the thumb out.

The rumor is that after Willard had made his many and individual studies of Mosher, that Mosher was unable to get to Cleveland to see the finished canvas of "The Spirit of '76." He did not see it until he visited the Centennial.

At the Centennial there was always a crowd around the painting. Mosher joined the crowd. While he thus stood before the picture, someone in the crowd recognized him, and he was immediately given an ovation.

One of the original sketches for the fifer, I believe, still exists. It was in existence and exhibited in Cleveland, November, 1912. At the same time also was exhibited a marble figure of the old drummer, Willard's father.

The Drummer Boy

HENRY KELSEY DEVEREUX

who posed for the drummer boy. From an original portrait taken about 1878

The Drummer Boy—H. K. D.

In the original sketches for "Yankee Doodle," Willard depicted three grown men. When the humorous aspect faded from his conception, and he decided to depict his father seriously, he conceived the idea of including for his third figure a young lad instead of a grown man. In this way, the picture would present three generations of patriots, the grandfather in the center, the father at his side, and on his right, the grandson looking up into grandpa's face with confidence and admiration.

In 1875, there was organized in Cleveland, Brooks School, a preparatory school for boys from ten years upward. It was so named after its inceptor, the Reverend John Brooks, who lost his life in a most tragic manner while in Boston to secure a principal for the school. It was a military school. In 1876, it was domiciled in its building on Carnegie Avenue (then Sibley Street) near the present East Thirty-sixth street. The spirit of the boys in the school was very military. They had for instructor the late Captain F. A. Kendall, who served with distinction during the Civil War. Three companies composed the Brooks School Battalion. The first company composed of the older boys; the second, of the intermediate; and the third, of the smaller boys in both age and stature. For some reason the third company, in competitive drills, always won over the other two. This was due undoubtedly to the natural sympathy older people always have for the younger and smaller when in competition. I was captain of the Third Company and it was my observation that the little fellows usually got most of any sympathy being given, yet, too, it was a noticeable fact that they tried harder, paid closer attention, and usually drilled more perfectly than the older boys. On the sixth of March, 1876, the Brooks School Battalion gave a competitive drill at their armory, in compliment to the Cleveland Grays, and as may be guessed every boy was on his toes to show the hero soldiers in gray what could be done. Mr. Willard, desiring a subject to use in his picture as a drummer boy, attended this drill. Why he selected me never has been explained to me. Maybe an incident in the drill of the Third Company had its effect. Anyway, to this day, although nearly fifty years have passed, recalling the happenings of that day brings to me a thrill for the earnest effort and perfection of drill of those little fellows. The two companies of larger boys had passed through their drill in a way to please everybody. When it came time for the little fellows to march out, every boy was keyed to the limit. They went through the set maneuvers perfectly and when about finished, it popped into my head to try something very difficult that the others had not tried. Marching down the side of the hall in column of fours, and wheeling to the left, at the end I gave the order "fours left into line and forward guide right double-quick march." So perfect was the spacing between the fours that they wheeled into line in perfect alignment, broke into double quick as one, and went charging down the hall toward the spectators amid a burst of applause. That settled the day and the Third Company retained the honor of being the color company.

One thing that likely intensified this military spirit among us was the fact that just at this time there was on exhibition at Cleveland, a panorama of the Battle of Lookout Mountain. It was a splendid picture, aroused much enthusiasm, and the proceeds—in part at least—went to pay for the completion of the soldier's monument at Dayton. A select squad from the Brooks School Battalion gave an exhibition drill in front of the picture to help the entertainment.

Shortly after this competitive drill, my father told me he had given permission to Mr. Willard to use me as a model for the drummer boy in his picture. I recall a feeling of resentment on my part for that meant giving up afternoon play, a thing not to be contemplated with a feeling of joy by any boy. However, paternal edicts generally prevail, and a beginning was made by going down to Mr. Ryder's gallery and posing for a number of photos. This was followed by a number of visits to Willard's studio where hours were passed in rather a trying way for a boy. Willard was very kind and thoughtful. He entertained me with stories of the war, told me what was in his mind for the creation of this picture, and often would let me rest and walk in front of the picture to see what he had done. I can recall the enthusiasm of the man. He worked as if possessed of an idea that pleased him, but which he might lose. With watching him work and the picture develop, I too soon became enthusiastic. I forgot that it was tiresome to stand on one leg, and that bent, the other advanced, and the foot resting on an inverted box, with the head twisted to one side and the eyes raised and arms outstretched, although it was really very exacting of one's temper and strength. However, things progressed rapidly, and by the thirtieth of March the picture was about finished, and I took my mother, at Willard's request to see it. I am sure she experienced the feeling that thousands of our mothers have when they have seen their beloved son marching off to war. And then the momentous day came when it was rolled up and sent to the Centennial.

That fall I went to the Centennial with my parents. We spent about two weeks there. Almost every day I went into the Art Gallery to stand before "The Spirit of '76." Each time I felt something aroused in me that did not diminish by the frequent visits. It also was curious to mark the effect on others. Always there was a crowd in front of the picture and many if not most of the people had perceptible tears rise to their eyes as they stood and gazed. Many actually cried, yet came again and again to look with reverence on that canvas that pulsed so much of American spirit.

Later in life I stood before the picture again, where it now hangs in Abbot Hall, Marblehead, Mass., for which town my father, Colonel John Henry Devereux, bought the picture and presented it thereto. Then, as before, not only to me but to all in the room, arose a feeling of sentiment, a feeling of reverence, a feeling almost of awe that made one instinctively bare one's head and swallow the lump that will sometimes come in one's throat.

It may be that enthusiasm borne of an intimate knowledge of the creation of this picture makes me over-enthusiastic, but then and afterwards, even to this day, when I learn how it holds the interest of all that look at it, the belief is strengthened that the picture was an inspiration, though it might be judged crude in execution by artistic standards. I know little or nothing of art, nor does the ordinary individual looking at a picture, but any one picture that can so universally move the onlooker must convey something deeper than the pigments on the canvas. The determination and fight depicted by the old man in face and figure, without uniform, in shirt sleeves, coat off, sleeves loose, vest open and shirt open at throat without collar or stock is symbolical of the patriot ready to fight without purchase or thought of anything but the cause at heart. The fifer, a touch of humor for his, a humorous face, his fringe of whiskers, but a bandage about his head on which blood shows, a twinkle in his eye, but a set look on the face and a decided poise in the figure marching to his own fife music. The boy fresh from a loving mother's care and carefully uniformed, his eyes fixed upon his adored grandsire that he may do all that this loved, brave, and loyal man is determined to do. The wounded soldier in the foreground, his head pillowed on the shell-shattered wheel of a cannon, with heart and strength enough left to raise his cap in salute to "Old Glory." Over them all the flag of freedom, the stars and stripes, back of which come the first line of cheering patriotic troops entering action. It tells the story of the old way, and of the spirit and determination when men fought face to face, each individual a fighting machine to fight for love of country and freedom.

The flag is really an anachronism, as although it depicts the thirteen stripes and the thirteen stars on a blue field, it was not until June, 1777, that the United State Congress really accepted this design, and Betsy Ross made the first flag with these emblems.

The painting created little or no stir among the art critics and connoisseurs. It was not painted for such. The painting was a patriotic human document that reached the hearts of millions and will for centuries to come be an inspiration to further millions yet unborn.

Archibald M. Willard has passed. He may not be classed as a great artist but in the "Spirit of '76" he painted himself into everlasting fame.

An Early Account

THE REVEREND SAMUEL WILLARD
who posed for the central figure in the painting

An Early Account by J. F. Ryder

The conception and purpose of the artist and his adviser cannot be better interpreted than in Mr. Ryder's own words, written many years ago.

"The idea of the artist in painting the picture was to concentrate all the determination and enthusiasm possible in a few figures. No field afforded a better subject than the Revolution, with its determined old heroes and the air of 'Yankee Doodle' to rouse them to the highest pitch of enthusiasm.

"The three chief figures meet all the requirements of the situation and are in true keeping with the surroundings. Over them lower the clouds of smoke from a battle-field toward which they are marching. Behind them a few brave Continentals struggle up the hill, while by the side of a dismantled cannon lies a wounded soldier who raised himself on his elbow to give a last cheer to the stirring strains of 'Yankee Doodle.' The lines have evidently been forced back. The dying soldier and the broken cannon show where the line has stood. The other soldiers have been retreating. But the three musicians advance, and the sound of their music thrills the retreating troops with new courage. Hats are in the air; the flag has turned; the threatened defeat is about to become a victory. The dying man raised himself to cheer. The trio of homespun musicians are discoursing with all their might that music whose shrill melody is so surcharged with patriotism. The old drummer in the centre, bare-headed, grand in his fearlessness, without coat, one sleeve rolled up as though he had turned from the plough to grasp the drumsticks, his white hair blown in the air, his eyes set close and defiant as though he saw the danger and feared it not, the sharp lines about his mouth showing a fixed determination—all combine to make up that wonderful figure in our history which no rags could degrade nor splendor ennoble—the Continental soldier.

"On the left of the brave old drummer is the fifer who seems to have come to blow his fife, and he will do it as well here among the flying bullets as in the porch of his cottage. His eyes are fixed toward the sky as though reading the notes of his music on the clouds. Around his brow is a bloodstained handkerchief, which tells of the bullet which grazed yet spared him. His whole energy is poured into the reed at his lips, and one can almost hear the shrill notes of 'Yankee Doodle' above the noise of battle.

"On the right of the old man marches a boy, hardly in his teens, whose drum keeps time to the beat of the other. His face is upturned to the old man, as though he were his grandfather, as if to question perhaps the route or the danger ahead, but still with a look of rapt inspiration. No shade of fear lurks in his calm eyes, while the 'rub-a-dub' of his little drum sounds as clear and distinct as the heavier roll of the aged drummer.

"The entire group is conceived with a fervid sympathy which makes the observer concede sure victory to the combatants; victory also to the artist. The man who had carried the stars and stripes, marching under the same thrilling tune, put his heart into the picture. The work was an inspiration. Mr. Willard had no thought of depicting three generations of one family, but the inference is so natural that he has cheerfully adopted it.

"The canvas is large and figures are heroic in size. When finished, the picture was placed in the show window of my art store in Cleveland. The crowds which gathered about it blockaded the entrance to the gallery and obstructed the sidewalk to such an extent that it was necessary to remove it from the window to the rear of the store, where it was on exhibition for several days, during which time all business in the store was discontinued on account of the crowds which filled the place. The interest and enthusiasm which it created were remarkable. The late Right Reverend

Bishop Bedell was a daily visitor and frequently spent an entire half day, so deeply was he impressed.

"The painting was finally sent to the Centennial Exposition at Philadelphia and prominently placed in Memorial Hall, where it created a notable interest throughout the Exposition. After which by earnest request it was taken to Boston and exhibited for several weeks in the Old South Meetinghouse. Thence it was taken to the Corcoran Gallery at Washington, thence to Chicago, San Francisco, and other cities, always by request—so great was the desire of the public to see the painting which had aroused such enthusiasm in the hearts of a patriotic people. At last it found a permanent home in Abbot Hall at Marblehead, Mass., the gift to that old town of the late General J. H. Devereux, who purchased it from Willard to present it to the town of his birth. It stands in the old hall which breathes of historic patriotism. It is the pride of the people of Marblehead and of all Americans who visit it.

"Pictures have been painted by artists of great skill, possessing qualities of technique of method, valuable beyond the works of other artists; pictures which give pleasure to experts and connoisseurs. In the midst of such works 'The Spirit of '76' stands. The eye wanders from these works of great technique, and is awed by the grandeur of the old man, by the force of the fervid and devoted group, by the spirit which invades the whole. Mr. Willard with his powerful but, perhaps, less finished touch did more than please the eye of experts; he stirred the heart of a nation."

Preliminary Sketches and Replicas

THE FINAL PRELIMINARY CRAYON STUDY SKETCH

Showing one of the stages in the evolution of the finished painting. Believed to be the only study sketch now in existence

The Preliminary Sketches and Replicas

A number of preliminary sketches were made. Of these, I believe, only one is now in existence. It is owned by the Reverend William E. Barton of Oak Park, Illinois, who was formerly pastor of the First Congregational Church at Wellington, Ohio. It came into Doctor Barton's possession in the following manner. In the preparation of his early sketches for the preliminary groupings, Mr. Willard was assisted by Mr. William F. Sawtelle, a photographer of Wellington. Willard gave this original crayon sketch to Mr. Sawtelle. Mr. Sawtelle preserved it, expecting to pass it on to his son. His son died. Mr. Sawtelle was a member of Doctor Barton's church. Upon the death of his son, Mr. Sawtelle gave this crayon sketch to Doctor

Barton. This original rough sketch embodies essentially the ideas wrought out in the oil painting, but naturally it is rough and unfinished. The drummer boy is a head shorter. His face is in the shadow. The dying man is much too prominent in the foreground, a mistake which Willard later corrected. Apart from these points, it lacks altogether the spirit and inspiration which Willard worked into his finished painting.

Apart from the preliminary sketch referred to in the preceding paragraph, Doctor Barton possesses an original painting of "The Spirit of '76" made by Mr. Willard. This Willard executed in oils and in size thirty-four by twenty-eight inches. This painting was made in 1916 and really constitutes the third and last original painting of "The Spirit of '76" made by Mr. Willard. The original and the Cleveland replica are full size. This third painting is really executed in miniature. Willard did not attempt to make an exact copy; hence, in this small painting there are many variations from the two larger paintings. It was presented to Doctor Barton. It was painted by Mr. Willard to replace a large photograph of "The Spirit of '76" which was hanging in Doctor Barton's home during one of Mr. Willard's visits. Doctor Barton's home then being in Oak Park, Illinois. The Reverend William E. Barton was for many years a close personal friend of Mr. Willard, and conducted his funeral services. Mr. Willard died at 4933 Holyoke Avenue, Cleveland, October 11, 1918. The funeral services were held in Cleveland, but the burial was in the Willard lot, among his old friends at Wellington, Ohio.

Doctor Barton also possesses probably the only original sketch made to convey Willard's original conception of what he intended to call "Yankee Doodle," the idea of which was entirely changed after he met and talked with Ryder, and a patriotic instead of a humorous conception was decided on. Doctor Barton had asked Willard if he had any of his first sketches that were humorous, to which Willard had replied that he had not preserved any of these. Doctor Barton then asked him whether he had the original idea of the Fourth of July celebration which he had intended to call "Yankee Doodle" sufficiently in mind to make for Doctor Barton a sketch which would embody Willard's original conception for the painting. Willard replied that he had this original idea well in mind and would be glad to make for Doctor Barton a crayon sketch thereof. A little later Willard made this and in sending this to Doctor Barton, with characteristic humor entitled it "The First Sketch that was made Last." This sketch does not typify "The Spirit of '76." It is merely the forerunner out of which "The Spirit of '76" was evolved. It is strictly a humorous sketch of Fourth of July musicians marching. The wonderful inspiration developed in "The Spirit of '76" is entirely lacking. This Willard made for Doctor Barton in 1898.

In 1912 a replica of "The Spirit of '76" was made by Willard himself. Willard was then 76 years of age. This replica was executed for the City of Cleveland as a special Commission. This is located in a prominent place in the new City Hall at Cleveland. It is fitting that this replica should be available in Cleveland where "The Spirit of '76" was conceived and executed by a Cleveland artist and painted from Cleveland and northern Ohio subjects. This replica naturally is not as well executed as the original. This would be almost impossible at Willard's then advanced age. In this replica Willard incorporated a number of changes. The coloring is different. He changed the arrangement of the stars from a circle of thirteen stars to a circle of nine with four stars in the center. He moderated the stride of the men. He changed the wounded soldier in the foreground to a more upright position. He changed the drummer boy. The drummer boy who posed in the Cleveland replica was Willard's grandson, Williard Connelly, a Cleveland Central High School boy.

In 1917, another artist, James M. Flagg, painted a picture which he entitled "The Spirit of 1917" for which he took Willard's idea, painting the men to look younger and putting them into modern uniforms, making a few other changes and then taking credit for having originated the picture.

Milton Keynes UK
Ingram Content Group UK Ltd.
UKHW050648260624
444769UK00004B/165